D1795636

NZ TIME

That was the big effect Lord of the Rings had on me. It was discovering New Zealand. And even more precious were the people not at all like the Australians. Ian Mckellen

CPSIA information can be obtained
at www.ICGtesting.com
Printed in the USA
BVHW090852240719
554235BV00020B/725/P

9 780464 032427